Faith
Begins

⌘

edited and compiled
by Dr. Jeffrey P. Johnson

FAITH BEGINS
edited and compiled by Dr. Jeffrey P. Johnson
with assistance from Erin Smith

cover design by Erin Eckberg

Scripture quotations are taken from the THE HOLY BIBLE, NEW
INTERNATIONAL VERSION®, NIV® Copyright © 1973, 1978,
1984, 2011 by Biblica, Inc.™ Used by permission. All rights reserved
worldwide.

All hymns included are public domain but were gleaned from *The
Hymnal for Worship and Celebration,* Word Music, 1986.

ISBN 0-89367-303-X
13 Digit ISBN 978-0-89367-303-1

© 2011, reprint 2014
For Men's Ministries International
By Light and Life Communications
Indianapolis, Indiana
Printed in the U.S.A.

DEDICATION

This book is dedicated to Ian Wesley Johnson, Caleb Michael Smith and Jackson Paul Mazzei, who are sons of light and hope for the 21st century. May God bless you as your faith begins, and may the Lord Jesus Christ guard and perfect your faith until it becomes sight.

This is the message we have heard from him and declare to you: God is light; in him there is no darkness at all. If we claim to have fellowship with him yet walk in the darkness, we lie and do not live by the truth. But if we walk in the light, as he is in the light, we have fellowship with one another, and the blood of Jesus, his Son, purifies us from all sin.
    1 John 1:5-7

Let no one deceive you. God is light, and to those who have entered into union with him, he imparts of his own brightness to the extent that they have been purified.
    Symeon the New Theologian
    949-1022

INTRODUCTION

The purpose of this book is to help new Christians form their life of faith in Jesus Christ. A balanced spiritual life requires participation in the kingdom of God and in a community of faith. The problem is that most new Christians receive very little training when they first place their faith in Jesus, and many become discouraged, confused and even walk away from church and Christ.

The Bible is the Word of God and a revelation of who God is. This revelation is an invitation to join his kingdom. God moves first, God speaks first and God initiates faith first, and it is up to the person to respond to God's gracious calling. Faith in God starts with the holy and enters the ordinary.

Faith is about being discovered, being loved and being understood. It requires a change in approach from the mind (to seek, to understand, to love) to the heart (to be found, to be understood, to be loved). It includes the personality and character of the person who believes and the willingness to let Jesus Christ enter his or her life and create a sacred place. By faithful obedience new Christians become disciples (followers) and begin the transformation process. They accept the grace of God and apply it to their lives. They pattern their lives after Jesus by seeking to imitate his life, his attitude, his simplicity and his love. As disciples they allow the Holy Spirit to transform them from the inside out and recreate them in the likeness of Jesus Christ.

A life of faith is not an instant act or moment. No one is zapped into the image of Christ. It takes time to learn and process. It requires periods of living and dying, preparation and growth. Every area of peoples' lives need to be touched by the grace of God. They learn to be honest with God, honest with themselves and honest with others. Faith must be real, tangible and dynamic. The goal of faith is to bring

salvation to the soul, and this includes holiness and whole-
ness in Jesus Christ. As people live and move in Christ, they
discover the freedom that comes from faith. They learn that
by faith they can survive tests, trials and temptations. It is
faith that keeps them close to the heart of God. It is faith that
learns to trust God. It is faith that moves them from a set of
convictions and beliefs to an interactive relationship of love
and commitment. A simple faith can go a long way in the
kingdom of God, and every disciple must exercise his or her
faith in Jesus Christ.

Enjoy the next 40 days, and may God bless you as you
follow Jesus Christ. Each day will start with a Bible verse
from the Gospel of Mark, followed a brief devotional read-
ing, and end with a prayer from the Psalms.

Each week will include some helpful hints on the faith
journey and some general aids in understanding the Bible.
At the back of the book are some affirmations of faith from
the Bible and early church history.

- ◆ The Gospel (good news) of Mark is one of four
  gospels that gives a biographical sketch of the
  life, ministry, death and resurrection of Jesus
  Christ. The other gospels are Matthew, Luke and
  John. Matthew and John were disciples of Jesus
  Christ; Luke was a physician and later on wrote;
  Mark was a young man who lived in Jerusalem
  and was active in the early church. Matthew,
  Mark and Luke follow the same pattern and are
  called the Synoptic Gospels, while John writes
  in a different manner following the same major
  events.

- ◆ The Psalms are a collection of prayers, songs
  and praises from the Jewish people and their
  faith journey with God. They have been used

as a guide for prayer for more than 5,000 years and contain a variety of expressions of the faith including joy, sadness, suffering, victory, confession and thanksgiving. There are 150 psalms in the Bible.

Psalm 1

Blessed is the one
who does not walk in step with the wicked
*   or stand in the way that sinners*
take or sit in the company of mockers,
*   but whose delight is in the law of the LORD,*
and who meditates on his law day and night.
*   That person is like a tree planted by streams of water,*
which yields its fruit in season
*   and whose leaf does not wither —*
whatever they do prospers.

Not so the wicked!
They are like chaff
that the wind blows away.
Therefore the wicked will not stand in the judgment,
nor sinners in the assembly of the righteous.

For the LORD watches over the way of the righteous,
but the way of the wicked leads to destruction.

DAY 1

After John was put in prison, Jesus went into Galilee, pro-claiming the good news of God. "The time has come," he said. "The kingdom of God is near. Repent and believe the good news!"
Mark 1:14-15

Jesus talked about God in a new and different way. He spoke about the "good news" of God, which included God's love, God's faithfulness and God's goodness. Jesus taught that God is gracious, compassionate, slow to anger, rich in love, and good to all (*Psalm 145:8-9*). Most people think God is distant and does not care about what happens to us. Other people believe God is harsh and makes life difficult. Jesus said "God is near" and we could come close and experience the grace and goodness.

Jesus gave two conditions on starting a relationship with God. First, we must repent, which means we stop what we are doing and turn toward God. When we repent, we change our thinking; we change our direction; and we change our attitude. We turn toward God and believe the good stuff about God. We accept God's love; we welcome God's faithfulness; and we trust in God's goodness. We repent and then believe. When we believe the good news of God we are opening a door for him to work in and through us. We are beginning the journey of faith.

Read *Psalm 2*, which God promises to be with us and help us in times of trouble.

DAY 2

Very early in the morning, while it was still dark, Jesus got up, left the house and went off to a solitary place, where he prayed.
    Mark 1:35

Jesus had a relationship with God and did things that helped the relationship grow. Jesus was baptized by John in the Jordan River as an act of obedience (*Mark 1:9*); Jesus fasted for 40 days in the desert as an act of discipline (*Mark 1:12-13*); Jesus shared the good news of God with others as an act of love (*Mark 1:16-18*); Jesus healed people who were troubled and sick as an act of mercy (*Mark 1:21-34*); and Jesus prayed to God daily in the morning as an act of righteousness (*Mark 1:35*). All these things helped Jesus trust in God's love, God's faithfulness and God's goodness.

Jesus once said we are not to do our "acts of righteousness" in front of people to look good or think we are better than others (*Matthew 6:1*). Instead we are to seek God in ways that honor him and respect others. God wants everyone to experience his goodness and grace, and we must be careful not to push them away by what we say or do. Our relationship with God through Jesus Christ is directly connected to our relationship with others. When we love God, we also must love others.

Read *Psalm 3*, which is a prayer for help and deliverance from evil.

John the Baptist

Miracle Birth — *Luke 1:5-25*
1. Father: Zechariah — a priest in the temple at Jerusalem
2. Mother: Elizabeth — related to Mary the mother of Jesus
3. Parents were old in age — *remember Abraham and Sarah*
4. John's birth foretold by an angel (Gabriel) in the temple
5. Gabriel gives instructions about John's name
6. Zechariah argued with Gabriel and was made mute until John's birth
7. Mary and Elizabeth meet in the hill country of Judea — *Luke 1:39-45*
8. Zechariah is filled with the Holy Spirit when John is circumcised — *Luke 1:57-80*

Prophetic Ministry — *Mark 1:1-8*
1. John the Baptist appears in all four Gospels
2. John is on a preaching mission down by the Jordon River
3. Preaches repentance and baptism for the forgiveness of sins — confession
4. John eats locust and wild honey and wears simple clothing
5. Large crowds come to hear him, and even Christ is baptized by him
6. Criticizes Herod Antipas for his marriage to his brother's wife — *Matthew14:3*
7. John arrested and beheaded by Herod because of an oath — *Matthew 14:1-12*
8. John's influence lasts for more than 20 years — *Acts 18:25; 19:1-7*

DAY 3

A few days later, when Jesus again entered Capernaum, the people heard that he had come home. So many gathered that there was no room left, not even outside the door, and he preached the word to them.

Mark 2:1-2

Many people were excited about Jesus coming to their town because he helped them learn more about God. He also healed many people who had various diseases (*Mark 1:32-34*). Some people had trouble in their mind; others had trouble in their body; and some even had trouble in their spirit; but when Jesus touched them, they were changed. They experienced the power of God through the compassion of Jesus Christ (*Mark 1:41*).

Jesus also forgive people of their sins. Sin is a thought, word or action that hurts God, others or even ourselves. When we think something bad, or say something bad or do something bad, it is a sin. Sin separates us from God and others, and makes us feel guilty and shameful. Many times we know we have sinned but do not know how to find forgiveness. Because Jesus Christ is the Son of God, he has the ability to forgive people their sins and help them be right with God and others. This is part of the good news of God. Not everyone was happy about this. Many religious leaders thought only God could forgive sins (*Mark 2:6-7*), and so Jesus healed a person by forgiving the person's sins (*Mark 2:8-12*). Everyone was amazed.

Read *Psalm 4*, which encourages us to hope in God and develop patient endurance.

DAY 4

*While Jesus was having dinner at Levi's house, many tax col-
lectors and "sinners" were eating with him and his disciples, for
there were many who followed him. When the teachers of the law
who were Pharisees saw him eating with the "sinners" and tax
collectors, they asked his disciples: "Why does he eat with tax collectors and 'sinners'?"*

*On hearing this, Jesus said to them, "It is not the healthy who
need a doctor, but the sick. I have not come to call the righteous,
but sinners."*

Mark 2:15-17

Jesus asked people to help him share the good news of
God. These men and women were called disciples or followers. A disciple is a person who thinks and acts like his or
her teacher. Jesus had many disciples who followed him but
selected 12 to be called "apostles" (*Mark 3:13-19*). An apostle
is a person who is "sent" on mission — the 12 apostles were
on a mission to share the good news of God.

When Jesus asked Levi (also called Matthew) to become
a disciple some people were not happy. Levi had been a bad
person, and people did not like him. When Jesus came by he
gave Levi a choice: to change his life by following him or to
stay in the same place, doing the same thing. Levi decided
to follow Jesus and become a disciple. Levi repented and
believed in the good news of God. Levi put his faith in God
and received the forgiveness of his sins. He was a changed
person. He was a new man. He was transformed from the
inside out. Years later Levi would write about the life and
work of Jesus in what we call the Gospel of Matthew.

Read *Psalm 5*, which warns those who think and do evil
things. It encourages God's people to be holy and do the
right things at the right time.

Books of the New Testament

GOSPELS
Matthew   Mark   Luke   John

HISTORY
Acts of the Apostles

LETTERS OF PAUL   **GENERAL LETTERS**
Romans   Hebrews
1 and 2 Corinthians   James
Galatians   1 and 2 Peter
Ephesians   1, 2 and 3 John
Philippians   Jude
Colossians
1 and 2 Thessalonians
1 and 2 Timothy
Titus
Philemon

APOCALYPTIC LITERATURE
Revelation

DAY 5

Jesus withdrew with his disciples to the lake, and a large crowd from Galilee followed. When they heard all he was doing, many people came to him from Judea, Jerusalem, Idumea, and the regions across the Jordan and around Tyre and Sidon. Because of the crowd he told his disciples to have a small boat ready for him, to keep the people from crowding him.
Mark 3:7-9

Everywhere Jesus went he shared the good news of God, helped people find forgiveness of their sins, and challenged the religious leaders to be more loving and kind. Jesus was upset because the religious leaders had stubborn hearts and did not want to believe the good news (*Mark 3:5-6*). They even made plans to kill Jesus; but this did not stop Jesus from his mission.

People came from many places to hear Jesus preach, teach and to be healed. Jesus was doing something new, and new things make some people afraid (*Mark 2:21-22*). Some people have a fear of the unknown and do not want to risk what they already have. Some people have a fear of failure and do not want to be embarrassed or look bad. Some people have a fear of rejection and do not feel loved, accepted or approved. Wherever Jesus went, he helped people overcome their fears and put their trust in the love of God. God's perfect love removes our fears and helps us live in a new way.

Read *Psalm 6*, which is a prayer asking for forgiveness and mercy.

DAY 6

Jesus went up on a mountainside and called to him those he wanted, and they came to him. He appointed twelve — designating them apostles — that they might be with him and that he might send them out to preach and to have authority to drive out demons.
  Mark 3:13-15

Many people followed Jesus including men, women and children. Jesus asked 12 men to be with him and learn more about the good news of God. Jesus showed them the power of God's love and sent them to tell others about his love. They preached the forgiveness of sins through the acceptance of God's love and the deliverance of evil through the presence of God's love.

These were ordinary men who heard the call of God and obeyed the will of God. They were fishermen, tax collectors, farmers, husbands, brothers and sons. They learned from Jesus and then shared what they learned with others. It was not always easy because some people did not want to hear about forgiveness, mercy and grace. Some people do not want to change even when the changing is good for them.

Read *Psalm 7*, in which God warns those who do evil and encourages those who do what is right.

The Levels of Influence in the Mission of Jews

1. The Crowds — 4,000-5,000 people — preaching, teaching, healing, eating — *Matthew 14:13-21*
2. The 500 — saw the resurrected Christ before the Ascension — *1 Corinthians 15:3-8*
3. The 120 — waited in the Upper Room for the coming of the Holy Spirit — *Acts 1:12-2:4*
4. The 70 — appointed to go ahead of the Lord and prepare the way — *Luke 10:1-20*
5. The Women — Mary Magdalene, Joanna, Susanna and many others supporting Jesus — *Luke 8:1-3*
6. The Twelve — discipled by Jesus, preached and cast out demons — *Mark 3:13-18*
7. The Three — Peter, James and John spend time with Jesus — *Matthew 17:1-13*

The Twelve Disciples — *Luke 6:12-16*

1. Simon Peter — (reed/rock) — betrays Christ and later becomes Church leader — *Matthew 14:25-32*
2. Andrew — (manly) — Peter's brother and one of the first disciples — *John 1:35-42*
3. James — (supplanter) — John's brother; both have a fiery temper — *Luke 9:51-56*
4. John — (God is Gracious) — known as the beloved disciple — *John 21:20-23*
5. Philip — (lover of horses) — came from a Greek colony in Bethsaida — *John 12:20-22*
6. Bartholomew — (Nathaniel) (gift of God) — a true Israelite — *John 1:43-51*
7. Matthew — (Levi) (gift of God) — a tax collector who wrote a Gospel — *Matthew 9:9-13*
8. Thomas — (twin) — has a special appearance of the risen Christ — *John 20:24-29*

9. James Alphaeus — (supplanter) — only listed in Scriptures
10. Simon the Zealot* — (reed) — only listed in Scripture *(* Zealots opposed Roman occupation)*
11. Judas Thaddeus — (courageous praise) — asks a question at the Lord's Supper — *John 14:22-24*
12. Judas Iscariot — (praise from Cariot) — only Judean among the 12; betrayed Christ — *Acts 1:15-22*

The Duties of Disciples — *Luke 10:1-16*
1. Pray for the harvest of souls
2. Live simply — clothes, food, housing
3. Give a blessing
4. Heal the sick
5. Preach the kingdom
6. Ministry of word and prayer
7. Servants of Christ

DAY 7

Then Jesus' mother and brothers arrived. Standing outside,
they sent someone in to call him. A crowd was sitting around him,
and they told him, "Your mother and brothers are outside looking
for you."

"Who are my mother and brothers?" he asked.

Then he looked at those seated in a circle around him and said,
"Here are my mother and my brothers! Whoever does God's will is
my brother and sister and mother."

Mark 3:31-35

Jesus was faithful in telling people the good news of God even when his family was nearby. Jesus had four brothers (James, Joseph, Judas and Simon) and at least two sisters (*Mark 6:3*). Mary, the mother of Jesus, listened to God and through difficult situations obeyed the will of God. Mary was engaged to a man names Joseph from Nazareth in northern Israel (*Matthew 1:18*). She became pregnant when the Spirit of God overshadowed her (*Luke 1:35*) and gave birth to Jesus in a town called Bethlehem (*Luke 2:1-7*). Shortly after the birth of Jesus, the family moved to Egypt to avoid persecution and returned later (*Matthew 2:13-23*). Joseph is not mentioned again, but the brothers of Jesus — James and Judas — became leaders in the Jerusalem church after the resurrection. James is often called the elder (*1 Corinthians 15:3-8*) because he helped lead the Jerusalem church and was active in the first church council (*Acts 15:1-*29). Judas wrote a letter (*Jude*) encouraging the followers of Jesus to stand firm against false leaders and those who deny God altogether.

Read *Psalm 8*, which talks about the coming of Jesus and the majesty of his name.

DAY 8

He taught them many things by parables, and in his teaching said: "Listen! A farmer went out to sow his seed. As he was scattering the seed, some fell along the path, and the birds came and ate it up. Some fell on rocky places, where it did not have much soil. It sprang up quickly, because the soil was shallow. But when the sun came up, the plants were scorched, and they withered because they had no root. Other seed fell among thorns, which grew up and choked the plants, so that they did not bear grain. Still other seed fell on good soil. It came up, grew and produced a crop, multiplying thirty, sixty, or even a hundred times."
Mark 4:2-8

Jesus taught people the things of God by using parables. Parables are "earthly stories with heavenly wisdom" and often require some time to reflect and think to completely understand their meaning. Jesus also preached the good news of God when he sat down on a mountain in *Matthew 5:7-48;* Jesus revealed the good news of God when he turned water into wine at a wedding in *John 2:1-11;* and Jesus shared the good news of God when he healed the sick and set people free from evil spirits in *Luke 4:38-44.*

People learn in different ways by listening, watching, participating and imitating. God wants us to imitate Jesus — to think, speak, act and respond just like Jesus did. As followers of Jesus our goal is to become more like him and tell others about the good news of God.

Read *Psalm 9,* which encourages the followers of Jesus to trust in God's mercy and justice. God is a safe place in times of trouble.

DAY 9

*When he was alone, the twelve and the others around him
asked him about the parables. He told them, "The secret of the
kingdom of God has been given to you. But to those on the outside
everything is said in parables so that, 'they may be ever seeing but
never perceiving, and ever hearing but never understanding other-
wise they might turn and be forgiven!'*
Mark 4:10-12

Not everyone takes time to listen to God. Many people
fill their lives with other things and refuse to follow the way
of God. Some people think power is the only way to live this
life and take pride in what they can control. Other people
seek only pleasure, and everything they do, they do for their
own benefit. They become self-centered and lust after people
and things. Still other people believe that money will make
them happy and spend their entire life wanting more of it.
They put their trust in money, and greed becomes their moti-
vation for living.

Jesus said if we listen carefully to God and turn toward
the love of God, we would see and believe; we would hear
and understand; we would find forgiveness. The love of God
is greater than power, sex or even money. The love of God
can change the way people think and live.

Read *Psalm 10*, which is a prayer asking God for help
when evil people are causing trouble and hardship.

The Good Samaritan

On one occasion an expert in the law stood up to test Jesus. "Teacher," he asked, "what must I do to inherit eternal life?"

"What is written in the Law?" he replied. "How do you read it?"

He answered, "'Love the Lord your God with all your heart and with all your soul and with all your strength and with all your mind'; and, 'Love your neighbor as yourself.'"

"You have answered correctly," Jesus replied. "Do this and you will live."

But he wanted to justify himself, so he asked Jesus, "And who is my neighbor?"

In reply Jesus said: "A man was going down from Jerusalem to Jericho, when he was attacked by robbers. They stripped him of his clothes, beat him and went away, leaving him half dead. A priest happened to be going down the same road, and when he saw the man, he passed by on the other side. So too, a Levite, when he came to the place and saw him, passed by on the other side. But a Samaritan, as he traveled, came where the man was; and when he saw him, he took pity on him. He went to him and bandaged his wounds, pouring on oil and wine. Then he put the man on his own donkey, brought him to an inn and took care of him. The next day he took out two denarii and gave them to the innkeeper. 'Look after him,' he said, 'and when I return, I will reimburse you for any extra expense you may have.' "Which of these three do you think was a neighbor to the man who fell into the hands of robbers?"

The expert in the law replied, "The one who had mercy on him."

Jesus told him, "Go and do likewise."
Luke 10:25-37

Psalm 11

In the LORD I take refuge.
How then can you say to me:
"Flee like a bird to your mountain.
For look, the wicked bend their bows;
they set their arrows against the strings
to shoot from the shadows
at the upright in heart.
When the foundations are being destroyed,
what can the righteous do?"

The LORD is in his holy temple;
the LORD is on his heavenly throne.
He observes everyone on earth;
his eyes examine them.
The LORD examines the righteous,
but the wicked, those who love violence,
he hates with a passion.
On the wicked he will rain
fiery coals and burning sulfur;
a scorching wind will be their lot.

For the LORD is righteous,
he loves justice;
the upright will see his face.

DAY 10

Then Jesus said to them, "Don't you understand this parable? How then will you understand any parable? The farmer sows the word. Some people are like seed along the path, where the word is sown. As soon as they hear it, Satan comes and takes away the word that was sown in them. Others, like seed sown on rocky places, hear the word and at once receive it with joy. But since they have no root, they last only a short time. When trouble or persecution comes because of the word, they quickly fall away. Still others, like seed sown among thorns, hear the word; but the worries of this life, the deceitfulness of wealth and the desires for other things come in and choke the word, making it unfruitful. Others, like seed sown on good soil, hear the word, accept it, and produce a crop — thirty, sixty or even a hundred times what was sown."
Mark 4:13-20

Jesus explained this parable to his disciples, which is also found in *Matthew 13:9* and *Luke 8:48*. This seed is the Word of God, and it is shared with everyone, everywhere. God wants us to hear the Word and obey it just like Jesus. God wants us to grow in faith and learn to share the power of love with those around us.

When God's love grows in the followers of Jesus, it brings with it joy, peace, patience, kindness, goodness, gentleness, faithfulness and self-control (*Galatians 5:22-23*). We call these virtues the fruit of the Holy Spirit, because they benefit not only the followers of Jesus, but reflect the character and nature of God to all. To be like Jesus is to bear the fruit of the Holy Spirit in the love of God.

Read *Psalm 12*, which is a prayer for safety and protection. God comes to help those who are oppressed and in great need.

DAY 11

He said to them, "Do you bring a lamp to put it under a bowl or a bed? Instead, don't you put it on its stand? For whatever is hidden is meant to be disclosed, and whatever is concealed is meant to be brought out into the open. If anyone has ears to hear, let him hear."
Mark 4:21-23

Jesus is asking his followers to be a reflection of God's light in a dark world. Jesus wants us to live like we believe. If we believe in grace, then our lives should reflect grace. If we believe in truth, then our lives should reflect truth. If we believe in God, then our lives should reflect God in what we say, in what we do and in what we think.

God is good, and his followers must be good. God is just, and his followers must be just. God is holy, and his followers must be holy. Best of all God is love, and that means we must live in this amazing love, which has no height, no depth and no limit. Jesus showed the world that God's love never fails and never ends.

Read *Psalm 13*, which is a prayer when the followers of Jesus feel depressed and forgotten. God hears our prayer and shows us goodness and grace.

DAY 12

He also said, "This is what the kingdom of God is like. A man scatters seed on the ground. Night and day, whether he sleeps or gets up, the seed sprouts and grows, though he does not know how. All by itself the soil produces grain — first the stalk, then the head, then the full kernel in the head. As soon as the grain is ripe, he puts the sickle to it, because the harvest has come."
Mark 4:26-29

Jesus is teaching about the kingdom of God and uses another parable about seeds. This time the seed is sown, and after a while it grows and bears fruit. When people hear the Word of God it takes time for change to happen. This is called grace. God shows them love and goodness and then waits for them to respond. The Word of God stays with them and works from the inside out. It affects the way a person thinks and feels by bringing truth to his or her inner life. As grace and truth work together, the Word of God reveals what is right and what is wrong, and leads the person to do what is right. The person becomes a follower of Jesus when he or she looks and acts and sounds like Jesus.

Read *Psalm 14*, which warns against false teachers and those who do evil.

Amazing Grace

Amazing Grace, how sweet the sound,
That saved a wretch like me …
I once was lost but now am found,
Was blind, but now, I see.

T'was Grace that taught …
my heart to fear.
And Grace, my fears relieved.
How precious did that Grace appear …
the hour I first believed.

Through many dangers, toils and snares …
we have already come.
T'was Grace that brought us safe thus far …
and Grace will lead us home.

The Lord has promised good to me …
His word my hope secures.
He will my shield and portion be …
as long as life endures.

When we've been there ten thousand years …
bright shining as the sun.
We've no less days to sing God's praise …
then when we've first begun.

John Newton, John P. Rees, stanza 5,
Traditional

Psalm 15

LORD, who may dwell in your sacred tent?
Who may live on your holy mountain?
 The one whose walk is blameless,
who does what is righteous,
who speaks the truth from their heart;
 whose tongue utters no slander,
who does no wrong to a neighbor,
and casts no slur on others;
 who despises a vile person
but honors those who fear the LORD;
who keeps an oath even when it hurts,
and does not change their mind;
 who lends money to the poor without interest;
who does not accept a bribe against the innocent.

 Whoever does these things
will never be shaken.

DAY 13

*Again he said, "What shall we say the kingdom of God is like,
or what parable shall we use to describe it? It is like a mustard
seed, which is the smallest seed you plant in the ground. Yet when
planted, it grows and becomes the largest of all garden plants, with
such big branches that the birds of the air can perch in its shade."*
Mark 4:30-32

The kingdom of God starts in small ways and through
faith continues to grow and become the very cluster of who
we are. The first step is a simple prayer of surrender in
which we give God control of our lives. We declare that Jesus
is the Lord of what we do and what we say. As the kingdom
of God moves in us we find our hearts warmed by the presence of Jesus and a gently, holy peace comes over us.

The peace of God is a sign that God's love and God's
goodness are at work in us (*Romans 5:1-5*). We repent; we believe; and we have peace with God. To know God is to know
peace.

Read *Psalm 16*, which is a song for those who are suffering and facing death. It encourages the disciple to take
shelter in the presence of God.

DAY 14

A furious squall came up, and the waves broke over the boat, so that it was nearly swamped. Jesus was in the stern, sleeping on a cushion. The disciples woke him and said to him, "Teacher, don't you care if we drown?"

He got up, rebuked the wind and said to the waves, "Quiet! Be still!" Then the wind died down and it was completely calm.

He said to his disciples, "Why are you so afraid? Do you still have no faith?"

They were terrified and asked each other, "Who is this? Even the wind and the waves obey him!"

Mark 4:37-41

Life happens, and every day we face situations that can take away our peace and cause us to fear. That is why the followers of Jesus need to seek the grace of God in every moment. In *Psalm 5* we are encouraged to speak to God early in the morning with requests and prayers. In *Psalm 55* we are reminded to call upon God for help in the evening, morning and noon. In *Psalm 77* we are told to cry out to God in the night and that God will redeem us.

Read *Psalm 17*, which is a prayer against those who hate God and harm the disciples of Jesus.

Be Still My Soul

Be still, my soul: the Lord is on thy side.
Bear patiently the cross of grief or pain.
Leave to thy God to order and provide;
In every change, He faithful will remain.
Be still, my soul: thy best, thy heavenly Friend
Through thorny ways leads to a joyful end.

Be still, my soul: thy God doth undertake
To guide the future, as He has the past.
Thy hope, thy confidence let nothing shake;
All now mysterious shall be bright at last.
Be still, my soul: the waves and winds still know
His voice Who ruled them while He dwelt below.

Be still, my soul: when dearest friends depart,
And all is darkened in the vale of tears,
Then shalt thou better know His love, His heart,
Who comes to soothe thy sorrow and thy fears.
Be still, my soul: thy Jesus can repay
From His own fullness all He takes away.

Be still, my soul: the hour is hastening on
When we shall be forever with the Lord.
When disappointment, grief and fear are gone,
Sorrow forgot, love's purest joys restored.
Be still, my soul: when change and tears are past
All safe and blessed we shall meet at last.

Be still, my soul: begin the song of praise
On earth, be leaving, to Thy Lord on high;
Acknowledge Him in all thy words and ways,
So shall He view thee with a well pleased eye.
Be still, my soul: the Sun of life divine
Through passing clouds shall but more brightly shine.

Katharina von Schlegel,
Traditional

DAY 15

As Jesus was getting into the boat, the man who had been demon-possessed begged to go with him. Jesus did not let him, but said, "Go home to your family and tell them how much the Lord has done for you, and how he has had mercy on you." So the man went away and began to tell in the Decapolis how much Jesus had done for him. And all the people were amazed.
Mark 5:18-20

Jesus helps us to overcome our demons by loving us into a safe place. The love of God casts our fear and replaces it with righteousness, holiness and peace. This man had been in bondage, but the mercy of God set him free and Jesus encouraged him to go and tell others what had happened.

How do we face our demons? First, acknowledge the grace of God at work in our lives (*Colossians 3:15-17*). Second, pray for a fresh revelation of Jesus to give us light, life and peace (*Philippians 2:5-8*). Third, call upon the Holy Spirit to help us in our weakness (*Romans 8:26-27*). Fourth, turn to God and give Jesus control over every area of our lives (*1 John 1:9*). And finally, resolve to serve God in thought, word and action (*Acts 26:19-20*).

Read *Psalm 18*, which is a song of deliverance and praise for the character and nature of God.

DAY 16

*At once Jesus realized that power had gone out from him.
He turned around in the crowd and asked, "Who touched my
clothes?"*

*"You see the people crowding against you," his disciples an-
swered, "and yet you can ask, 'Who touched me?'"*

*But Jesus kept looking around to see who had done it. Then the
woman, knowing what had happened to her, came and fell at his
feet and, trembling with fear, told him the whole truth. He said to
her, "Daughter, your faith has healed you. Go in peace and be freed
from your suffering."*
Mark 5:30-34

The woman who touched Jesus had faith that God could
heal her. She believed and trusted in the power of God to
change her situation from being sick to being healthy. She
also had confidence that God would answer her prayer
through Jesus. Her faith produced an experience with the
living God that transformed her life.

How does faith work? Faith gives substance and meaning to hope (*Hebrews 11:1*). Faith is necessary to please God
and enter into a right relationship with God (*Hebrews 11:6*).
The followers of Jesus should make every effort to add to
their faith (*2 Peter 1:5-8*) and use the faith that God has given
them (*Romans 12:3*). Faith requires action (*James 2:22*) and
helps the followers of Jesus to overcome difficulties, hard-
ships and persecutions (*1 John 5:4*).

Read *Psalm 19*, which proclaims the coming of Jesus and
the power of the Word of God.

The Lord's Prayer

Our Father, who art in heaven, hallowed be thy name.
Thy Kingdom come, thy will be done,
on earth as it is in heaven.
Give us this day our daily bread.
And forgive us our sins,
as we forgive those who have sinned against us.
And lead us not into temptation,
but deliver us from evil.
For thine is the kingdom,
the power and the glory,
for ever and ever.
Amen.

    Matthew 6:9-13 (paraphrase)

DAY 17

While Jesus was still speaking, some men came from the house of Jairus, the synagogue ruler. "Your daughter is dead," they said. "Why bother the teacher any more?"

Ignoring what they said, Jesus told the synagogue ruler, "Don't be afraid; just believe."

He did not let anyone follow him except Peter, James and John the brother of James. When they came to the home of the synagogue ruler, Jesus saw a commotion, with people crying and wailing loudly. He went in and said to them, "Why all this commotion and wailing? The child is not dead but asleep." But they laughed at him.

After he put them all out, he took the child's father and mother and the disciples who were with him, and went in where the child was.
Mark 5:35-40

Faith makes a difference in the way we think, act, respond and even speak. Faith is not just a set of doctrines or a code of conduct or a spiritual experience. Faith is about following Jesus every day and becoming more like Jesus in every way. Faith is about committing everything to God — life, work, love, family and friends. It is about connecting to the Spirit of God through Jesus in order to become a people of grace, mercy and peace.

The followers of Jesus live by faith through conversion (*John 16:8-10*) and live for service through the power of the Holy Spirit (*1 Corinthians 12*). The followers of Jesus can connect to the present, forgive the past, hope of the future, overcome the worst and believe the best.

Read *Psalm 20*, which helps the followers of Jesus remember the blessings of God in the good times and the not-so-good times.

DAY 18

Jesus said to them, "Only in his hometown, among his relatives and in his own house is a prophet without honor." He could not do any miracles there, except lay his hands on a few sick people and heal them. And he was amazed at their lack of faith.
Mark 6:4-6

Some people lack the faith to trust in God. They deny the truth and ignore the goodness and grace of God around them. They avoid a commitment to God and seek to live life on their own terms. They repeat the same mistakes again and again hoping the next time will bring about change. They detach from God and from others in order to defend and preserve themselves.

Those who follow Jesus give God control of their lives. They become obedient to God's Word and live in God's will. They devote their resources for service to Jesus and the kingdom of God. They care for the needs of others showing honor, respect and love to everyone. They allow the Holy Spirit to move in them for worship and work. They help others find the goodness and grace of God in Jesus. They live by faith.

Read *Psalm 21*, which talks about the blessings that comes from Jesus including strength, life, joy and deliverance.

DAY 19

Calling the Twelve to him, he sent them out two by two and gave them authority over evil spirits.

These were his instructions: "Take nothing for the journey except a staff — no bread, no bag, no money in your belts. Wear sandals but not an extra tunic. Whenever you enter a house, stay there until you leave that town. And if any place will not welcome you or listen to you, shake the dust off your feet when you leave, as a testimony against them."

Mark 6:7-11

As followers of Jesus we have a duty to serve God and help other people. We have a life that comes from our faith in Jesus. We have a power from the presence of the Holy Spirit. We have a message of forgiveness to speak to the world. We have a sacrifice to give: our time, our talents, our treasurers. We have a revelation that comes from the resurrection of Jesus. We have a blessing that comes from the grace of God. We have a reward waiting for those who are faithful and true until the end.

When Jesus sent out his followers he was teaching them to obey God and listen to the Holy Spirit. He wanted them to learn to love God and to love people in grace and truth. Jesus wants us to learn how to love God and each other. Our mission is love.

Read *Psalm 22*, which tells about the suffering of Jesus on the cross and how God honors and redeems those sufferings.

Psalm 23

The LORD is my shepherd, I lack nothing.
He makes me lie down in green pastures,
he leads me beside quiet waters,
he refreshes my soul.
He guides me along the right paths
for his name's sake.
Even though I walk
through the darkest valley,
I will fear no evil,
for you are with me;
your rod and your staff,
they comfort me.
You prepare a table before me
in the presence of my enemies.
You anoint my head with oil;
my cup overflows.
Surely your goodness and love will follow me
all the days of my life,
and I will dwell in the house of the LORD forever.

DAY 20

The apostles gathered around Jesus and reported to him all they had done and taught. Then, because so many people were coming and going that they did not even have a chance to eat, he said to them, "Come with me by yourselves to a quiet place and get some rest."

So they went away by themselves in a boat to a solitary place.
Mark 6:30-32

Jesus showed his followers how to live a balanced life by teaching them how to rest. Jesus invited them to a quiet place where they could renew their strength and restore their souls. They were learning to set limits and boundaries for life and work. They were learning to schedule their time and that everything has a season (*Ecclesiastes 3:1-14*). They were learning to say "no" in order to fully obey God doing the right things at the right time.

God worked for six days and rested on the seventh day (*Genesis 2:2-3*). God declared the seventh day to be a day of rest, renewal and worship (*Exodus 20:9-10*). As followers of Jesus we need to balance work and rest, grace and trust, faith and action, life and ministry. We need to embrace life, work and love together, and learn to live within the paradox of heaven and earth.

Read *Psalm 24*, which is a song of praise about the coming of Jesus into the world.

DAY 21

But many who saw them leaving recognized them and ran on foot from all the towns and got there ahead of them. When Jesus landed and saw a large crowd, he had compassion on them, because they were like sheep without a shepherd. So he began teaching them many things.

By this time it was late in the day, so his disciples came to him. "This is a remote place," they said, "and it's already very late. Send the people away so they can go to the surrounding country-side and villages and buy themselves something to eat."

But he answered, "You give them something to eat."

They said to him, "That would take eight months of a man's wages! Are we to go and spend that much on bread and give it to them to eat?"

Mark 6:33-37

Jesus performed many miracles during his mission including miracles of healing, driving out demons, walking on water, silencing a storm and raising the dead to life again. A miracle occurs when God supernaturally intervenes in the nature world. The followers of Jesus believe God is always working in the world uncovering his goodness and grace. God was working in the Creation when everything came together, and it was good. God was working in the Incarnation when Jesus was sent from heaven. God was working in the Crucifixion when Jesus died on a cross for the sins of the world. God was working in the Resurrection when Jesus was raised from the dead. And God is working in the Consummation when all things will be complete, right and just. God is always working in the world.

Read *Psalm 25*, which tells the followers of Jesus how God will change their lives.

DAY 22

Again Jesus called the crowd to him and said, "Listen to me, everyone, and understand this. Nothing outside a man can make him 'unclean' by going into him. Rather, it is what comes out of a man that makes him 'unclean.'"
Mark 7:14-15

What we say and what we do makes us unclean. Jesus wants us to be honest to God and honest to ourselves as we follow him. The best way to honesty is by listening to God. When we listen to God it helps us to face our true condition. As we turn to God Jesus will set us free from our sins (*Romans 6:18*); free from our selfish ways (*Galatians 5:13*); free from our deception (*John 8:32*); free from ourselves (*John 8:36*); free from our fear of the law (*Romans 8:2*); free from our fear of authority (*Romans 13:3*); free from our accusers (*Colossians 1:22*); and free from our suffering (*Mark 5:34*).

As followers of Jesus we can live a new life, and we can speak words that bring new life. When our hearts are clean then we can love God, others and even self, with a holy and healthy love.

Read *Psalm 26,* which is a prayer for believing and doing the right things at the right time.

The Beatitudes

"Blessed are the poor in spirit,
for theirs is the kingdom of heaven.
Blessed are those who mourn,
for they will be comforted.
Blessed are the meek,
for they will inherit the earth.
Blessed are those who hunger
and thirst for righteousness,
for they will be filled.
Blessed are the merciful,
for they will be shown mercy.
Blessed are the pure in heart,
for they will see God.
Blessed are the peacemakers,
for they will be called children of God.
Blessed are those who are persecuted
because of righteousness,
for theirs is the kingdom of heaven.
Matthew 5:3-10

DAY 23

Jesus and his disciples went on to the villages around Caesarea Philippi. On the way he asked them, "Who do people say I am?"

They replied, "Some say John the Baptist; others say Elijah; and still others, one of the prophets."

"But what about you?" he asked. "Who do you say I am?"

Peter answered, "You are the Christ." Jesus warned them not to tell anyone about him.

Mark 8:27-30

Jesus asks his followers two questions: The first requires repetition only: "Who do the people say I am?" The second requires reflection: "Who do you say I am?" Every person must answer the second question. Every follower of Jesus must make a decision about who Jesus is and what Jesus wants.

If Jesus is the Christ (Messiah in Hebrew/Savior in English), then Jesus can change the way we think, the way we speak and the way we live. Jesus can form the life of faith in us by the grace of God. Jesus can teach us how to serve in the humility of God. Jesus can help us live like we believe to be a witness of God. Jesus can gather us together in a community of faith through the love of God.

Read *Psalm 27*, which is a prayer for trusting, seeking and waiting on the goodness of God.

DAY 24

Then he called the crowd to him along with his disciples and said: "If anyone would come after me, he must deny himself and take up his cross and follow me. For whoever wants to save his life will lose it, but whoever loses his life for me and for the gospel will save it. What good is it for a man to gain the whole world, yet forfeit his soul?"

Mark 8:34-36

When we follow Jesus, we must deny ourselves and take up the cross. We must count ourselves dead to sin and the world and alive to God (*Romans 6:11-14*). What does it mean to be dead to sin?

The following questions from Bishop Charles V. Fairbairn (Free Methodist, 1939-1961) might help us to deny ourselves and take up the cross of Jesus:

"Am I dead indeed to the glamour of the world?"

"Am I dead to the lure of worldly pleasure?"

"Am I dead to the decree of foolish and perhaps immodest fashion?"

"Am I dead to the opinions of my friends?"

"Am I dead to the scorn of my enemies?"

"Am I dead to the blame of the wicked?"

"Am I dead to the praise of the good?"

"Am I dead to the awful trend of the times?"

Read *Psalm 28*, which asks Jesus for mercy and gives thanks for the works of God.

Psalm 29

Ascribe to the LORD, you heavenly beings,
ascribe to the LORD glory and strength.
Ascribe to the LORD the glory due his name;
worship the LORD in the splendor of his holiness.
The voice of the LORD is over the waters;
the God of glory thunders,
the LORD thunders over the mighty waters.
The voice of the LORD is powerful;
the voice of the LORD is majestic.
The voice of the LORD breaks the cedars;
the LORD breaks in pieces the cedars of Lebanon.
He makes Lebanon leap like a calf,
Sirion like a young wild ox.
The voice of the LORD strikes
with flashes of lightning.
The voice of the LORD shakes the desert;
the LORD shakes the Desert of Kadesh.
The voice of the LORD twists the oaks
and strips the forests bare.
And in his temple all cry, "Glory!"
The LORD sits enthroned over the flood;
the LORD is enthroned as King forever.
The LORD gives strength to his people;
the LORD blesses his people with peace.

DAY 25

And he said to them, "I tell you the truth, some who are standing here will not taste death before they see the kingdom of God come with power."

After six days Jesus took Peter, James and John with him and led them up a high mountain, where they were all alone. There he was transfigured before them. His clothes became dazzling white, whiter than anyone in the world could bleach them. And there appeared before them Elijah and Moses, who were talking with Jesus.

Mark 9:1-4

Moses was a man God used to help set the Jewish people free from Egypt (*Exodus*). Elijah was a man God used to help the Jewish people remain faithful and true (*1 Kings 17*).

Moses and Elijah were prophets: people who see God and then speak God's Word. Moses taught the people the law of God (*Exodus 20*), and Elijah showed the people the will of God (*1 Kings 18:16-46*). They appear on the mountain with Jesus and his followers as Jesus prepares to go to Jerusalem to face death on a cross. The transfiguration is also recorded in *Matthew 17:1-13* and *Luke 9:28-36*.

Read *Psalm 30*, which is a song about how God turns our weeping into rejoicing.

Moses and the Burning Bush

Now Moses was tending the flock of Jethro his father-in-law, the priest of Midian, and he led the flock to the far side of the wilderness and came to Horeb, the mountain of God. There the angel of the LORD appeared to him in flames of fire from within a bush. Moses saw that though the bush was on fire it did not burn up. So Moses thought, "I will go over and see this strange sight — why the bush does not burn up."

When the LORD saw that he had gone over to look, God called to him from within the bush, "Moses! Moses!"

And Moses said, "Here I am."

"Do not come any closer," God said. "Take off your sandals, for the place where you are standing is holy ground." Then he said, "I am the God of your father, the God of Abraham, the God of Isaac and the God of Jacob." At this, Moses hid his face, because he was afraid to look at God. The LORD said, "I have indeed seen the misery of my people in Egypt. I have heard them crying out because of their slave drivers, and I am concerned about their suffering. So I have come down to rescue them from the hand of the Egyptians and to bring them up out of that land into a good and spacious land, a land flowing with milk and honey — the home of the Canaanites, Hittites, Amorites, Perizzites, Hivites and Jebusites. And now the cry of the Israelites has reached me, and I have seen the way the Egyptians are oppressing them. So now, go. I am sending you to Pharaoh to bring my people the Israelites out of Egypt."

Exodus 3:1-10

Elijah and the Presence of God

There he went into a cave and spent the night.

The LORD appears to Elijah and the word of the LORD came to him: "What are you doing here, Elijah?"

He replied, "I have been very zealous for the LORD God Almighty. The Israelites have rejected your covenant, torn down your altars, and put your prophets to death with the sword. I am the only one left, and now they are trying to kill me too."

The LORD said, "Go out and stand on the mountain in the presence of the LORD, for the LORD is about to pass by."

Then a great and powerful wind tore the mountains apart and shattered the rocks before the LORD, but the LORD was not in the wind. After the wind there was an earthquake, but the LORD was not in the earthquake. After the earthquake came a fire, but the LORD was not in the fire. And after the fire came a gentle whisper. When Elijah heard it, he pulled his cloak over his face and went out and stood at the mouth of the cave.

Then a voice said to him, "What are you doing here, Elijah?"

He replied, "I have been very zealous for the LORD God Almighty. The Israelites have rejected your covenant, torn down your altars, and put your prophets to death with the sword. I am the only one left, and now they are trying to kill me too."

The LORD said to him, "Go back the way you came, and go to the Desert of Damascus. When you get there, anoint Hazael king over Aram. Also, anoint Jehu son of Nimshi king over Israel, and anoint Elisha son of Shaphat from Abel Meholah to succeed you as prophet. Jehu will put to death any who escape the sword of Hazael, and Elisha will put to death any who escape the sword of Jehu. Yet I reserve seven thousand in Israel — all whose knees have not bowed down to Baal and whose mouths have not kissed him."

1 Kings 19:9-18

DAY 26

They left that place and passed through Galilee. Jesus did not want anyone to know where they were, because he was teaching his disciples. He said to them, "The Son of Man is going to be betrayed into the hands of men. They will kill him, and after three days he will rise." But they did not understand what he meant and were afraid to ask him about it.
Mark 9:30-32

Jesus tells his followers he will suffer, die and rise again in Jerusalem. The mission of Jesus started at his baptism when he showed his obedience to God and received the anointing of the Holy Spirit (*Luke 3:15-22*). Jesus set an example for everyone who would follow him. The mission of Jesus continued through his service to God, people and all creation (*Luke 22:27*). The mission of Jesus was based on his humility. He served God, and God sent him into the world. He emptied himself and laid down his life for others. He healed humanity with his suffering and death on a cross (*Philippians 2:6-18*). The mission of Jesus was completed in his resurrection. He defeated sin, death and hell. He set humanity free from sin and satisfied the needs of the law. Jesus kept his promise and brought justice to the world.

Read *Psalm 31*, which tells how Jesus put his trust and hope in the love of God.

DAY 27

Sitting down, Jesus called the Twelve and said, "If anyone wants to be first, he must be the very last, and the servant of all."

He took a little child and had him stand among them. Taking him in his arms, he said to them, "Whoever welcomes one of these little children in my name welcomes me; and whoever welcomes me does not welcome me but the one who sent me."

Mark 9:35-37

Jesus told his followers that if they wanted to be great, then they must become like children. Children are always learning and always growing. They are open, honest and do not hide behind words. They are relational, simple and trusting. Children live for love and love living.

As children of God we are called to walk in love, truth and obedience (*2 John 4-6*). We know God's love is made complete in us when we love others (*1 John 4:7-12*). We know that when we speak the truth in love it sets people free (*Ephesians 4:14-15*). We also know that when we obey God's Word and God's will, we bring honor to his name (*Colossians 3:17*).

Read *Psalm 32*, which teaches us about sin, confession and righteousness.

DAY 28

"Teacher," said John, "we saw a man driving out demons in your name and we told him to stop, because he was not one of us."

"Do not stop him," Jesus said. "No one who does a miracle in my name can in the next moment say anything bad about me, for whoever is not against us is for us. I tell you the truth, anyone who gives you a cup of water in my name because you belong to Christ will certainly not lose his reward."

Mark 9:38-41

Jesus has many followers, and we must be careful not to judge those working in his name. Those who follow Jesus will reflect the his character by loving God, doing good and avoiding evil. The followers of Jesus will show humility, faith, hope and love as they live their lives in peace. The followers of Jesus will grow in grace as they worship, pray, fast, study and fellowship together.

The mission of Jesus is to invite people to change the way they are living by turning to God and following Jesus. As they grow closer to God they are changed by his grace and empowered by his Spirit. They learn to trust, obey and serve in the goodness and grace of God.

Read *Psalm 33*, which is a song of praise and thanksgiving to God who gives the followers of Jesus hope.

DAY 29

People were bringing little children to Jesus to have him touch them, but the disciples rebuked them. When Jesus saw this, he was indignant. He said to them, "Let the little children come to me, and do not hinder them, for the kingdom of God belongs to such as these. I tell you the truth, anyone who will not receive the kingdom of God like a little child will never enter it." And he took the children in his arms, put his hands on them and blessed them.

Mark 10:13-16

Jesus blessed the children by giving them significance, strength and affirmation. Jesus affirmed their identity as participants in God's kingdom. Jesus strengthened their position by bringing them forward and blessing them. Jesus added significance to their lives by making them part of the mission.

The kingdom of God is for everyone: men, women, young, old. Anyone who turns to God and places his or her faith in Jesus can participate in the kingdom. How do we know they are in the kingdom? By the way they love God and love others.

Read *Psalm 34*, and learn about the goodness and love of God for those who put their hope in Jesus.

DAY 30

"I tell you the truth," Jesus replied, "no one who has left home or brothers or sisters or mother or father or children or fields for me and the gospel will fail to receive a hundred times as much in this present age (homes, brothers, sisters, mothers, children and fields — and with them, persecutions) and in the age to come, eternal life. But many who are first will be last, and the last first."
Mark 10:29-31

The Christian Journey

We believe in God the Father, who has made all things.
We believe in God the Son, who has redeemed all
    things.
We believe in God the Spirit, who has sanctified all
    things.
We live by faith through grace.
We live in holiness through obedience.
We live with understanding through Scripture.
We live to fellowship through the body of Christ.
We live for service through the power of God.
Amen.

Read *Psalm 35*, which is a prayer for those who do evil and forget the truth of God.

DAY 31

Jesus called them together and said, "You know that those who are regarded as rulers of the Gentiles lord it over them, and their high officials exercise authority over them. Not so with you. Instead, whoever wants to become great among you must be your servant, and whoever wants to be first must be slave of all. For even the Son of Man did not come to be served, but to serve, and to give his life as a ransom for many."
Mark 10:42-45

Steps of Humility

Step 1	Fearing God
Step 2	Loving the will of God
Step 3	Submitting to others
Step 4	Enduring affliction
Step 5	Confessing sins
Step 6	Finding peace and rest
Step 7	Becoming poor in spirit
Step 8	Living in community
Step 9	Controlling the tongue
Step 10	Learning to be serious
Step 11	Guarding against anger
Step 12	Taking the lower position

From the Rule of St. Benedict (modified)

Read *Psalm 36*, which warns the follower of Jesus to watch out for those who speak and do evil.

DAY 32

*"Have faith in God," Jesus answered. "I tell you the truth,
if anyone says to this mountain, 'Go, throw yourself into the sea,'
and does not doubt in his heart but believes that what he says will
happen, it will be done for him. Therefore I tell you, whatever you
ask for in prayer, believe that you have received it, and it will be
yours. And when you stand praying, if you hold anything against
anyone, forgive him, so that your Father in heaven may forgive you
your sins."*
Mark 11:22-25

The word faith comes from the Greek work *pistis*, which
means a strong conviction, dedication or commitment. The
followers of Jesus increase their faith by hearing the Word of
God (*Romans 10:17*). Faith does not rest on the wisdom of the
world (*1 Corinthians 2:5*) but develops through testing, trials
and temptations (*James 1:3*). Faith continues to grow in the
life of the followers of Jesus (*2 Corinthians 10:15*), and helps
them overcome problems in the world (*1 John 5:4*). Faith is
like a shield that protects those who follow Jesus (*Ephesians
6:16*).

When we pray by faith, God hears our prayers and helps
us in our situations. God shows us how to pray in the right
way and allows us to wait for the right time. God wants us
to be still and wait on him so we can reflect his love, mercy
and grace.

Read *Psalm 37*, which comforts the followers of Jesus by
learning to endure trusting in God.

DAY 33

Jesus replied, "Are you not in error because you do not know the Scriptures or the power of God? When the dead rise, they will neither marry nor be given in marriage; they will be like the angels in heaven. Now about the dead rising — have you not read in the Book of Moses, in the account of the burning bush, how God said to him, 'I am the God of Abraham, the God of Isaac, and the God of Jacob'? He is not the God of the dead, but of the living. You are badly mistaken!"
Mark 12:24-27

The Jewish people had many groups who believed different things about God. In this passage Jesus is talking to the *Sadducees* who believed in the law but not life after death (*Mark 12:18*). Jesus also talked with the *Pharisees* who believed in the law and added more laws to guard their righteousness (*Matthew 23:1-39*). Another group called the *Essenes* lived in communities and took vows of obedience. Some people think John the Baptist was part of this group (*Mark 1:1-8*). Another group was the *Zealots* who used fear and violence to get their way. Simon the Zealot was a follower of Jesus (*Luke 6:12-16*). The *Sanhedrin* was the Jewish religious court, which included the high priest, chief priests, elders, scribes and teachers (*Mark 14:53*).

Jesus challenges the *Sadducees* by declaring they do not understand the Word of God or power of God. Jesus tells them they are boldly mistaken in their views about God.

Read *Psalm 38*, which is a prayer of confession to God. God hears our prayers and brings comfort, strength and encouragement.

DAY 34

One of the teachers of the law came and heard them debating.
Noticing that Jesus had given them a good answer, he asked him,
"Of all the commandments, which is the most important?"
"The most important one," answered Jesus, "is this: 'Hear, O
Israel, the Lord our God, the Lord is one. Love the Lord your God
with all your heart and with all your soul and with all your mind
and with all your strength.' The second is this: 'Love your neighbor
as yourself.' There is no commandment greater than these."
Mark 12:28-31

Jesus reminds the people that love is the greatest thing in
the world. The followers' first love is for God alone: with all
their heart, soul, mind and strength. It is the highest priority
and brings the greatest reward. The second love is for others:
We use our eyes to see the people around us; we use our
hearts to feel what they feel; and we use our hands to serve
them in goodness and grace. The third love is for self; we
learn to love self with God's goodness and grace.

Sometimes we are our own worst enemy. We do not let
other people love us because we do not love ourselves. We
limit what God can do in us because we do not love ourselves. We must learn love from God and share that love
with others. As we live in love we will grow to love self.

Read *Psalm 39*, which brings comfort to the followers of
Jesus when we feel alone and rejected.

Psalm 40

I waited patiently for the LORD;
he turned to me and heard my cry.

He lifted me out of the slimy pit,
out of the mud and mire; he set my feet on a rock
and gave me a firm place to stand.

He put a new song in my mouth,
a hymn of praise to our God.

Many will see and fear
the LORD and put their trust in him.

Blessed is the one who trusts in the LORD,
who does not look to the proud,
to those who turn aside to false gods.

Many, LORD my God, are the wonders you have done,
the things you planned for us.

None can compare with you;
were I to speak and tell of your deeds,
they would be too many to declare.

Sacrifice and offering you did not desire —
but my ears you have opened —
burnt offerings and sin offerings you did not require.

Then I said, "Here I am, I have come —
it is written about me in the scroll.

I desire to do your will, my God;
your law is within my heart."

I proclaim your saving acts in the great assembly;
I do not seal my lips, LORD, as you know.

I do not hide your righteousness in my heart;
I speak of your faithfulness and your saving help.
I do not conceal your love and your faithfulness
from the great assembly.

Do not withhold your mercy from me, LORD;
may your love and faithfulness always protect me.

For troubles without number surround me;

my sins have overtaken me, and I cannot see.

 They are more than the hairs of my head,
and my heart fails within me.

 Be pleased to save me, LORD; come quickly,
LORD, to help me.

 May all who want to take my life
be put to shame and confusion;
may all who desire my ruin be turned back in disgrace.

 May those who say to me, "Aha! Aha!"
be appalled at their own shame.

 But may all who seek you rejoice and be glad in you;
may those who long for your saving help always
say, "The LORD is great!"

 But as for me, I am poor and needy;
may the Lord think of me. You are my help and
my deliverer; you are my God, do not delay.

DAY 35

"No one knows about that day or hour, not even the angels in heaven, nor the Son, but only the Father. Be on guard! Be alert! You do not know when that time will come. It's like a man going away: He leaves his house and puts his servants in charge, each with his assigned task, and tells the one at the door to keep watch.

"Therefore keep watch because you do not know when the owner of the house will come back — whether in the evening, or at midnight, or when the rooster crows, or at dawn. If he comes suddenly, do not let him find you sleeping. What I say to you, I say to everyone: 'Watch!'"

Mark 13:32-37

Jesus tells everyone to "watch!" The discipline of watching requires us to learn to be quiet. We must wait in stillness and silence in order to clearly see what is ahead of us. Watching also requires balance. We need to have boundaries in every area of our lives: work, rest, eating, drinking, playing and sleeping. We must embrace the rhythms of God's grace, which will keep us healthy and whole. Finally, the discipline of watching is connected to reflection and prayer. We need to open our hearts to the will of God and learn to think like Jesus. When we imitate Jesus in this way it helps us keep our hearts pure.

Jesus is coming back, and we must learn to be on guard and alert. We must learn to watch and pray. We must prepare our hearts and minds for his return.

Read *Psalm 41*, which tells about the rejection of Jesus and his betrayal by Judas Iscariot.

DAY 36

"Leave her alone," said Jesus. "Why are you bothering her?
She has done a beautiful thing to me. The poor you will always
have with you, and you can help them any time you want. But
you will not always have me. She did what she could. She poured
perfume on my body beforehand to prepare for my burial. I tell you
the truth, wherever the gospel is preached throughout the world,
what she has done will also be told, in memory of her."
Mark 14:6-9

This story is in all four Gospels in memory of the woman
who loved Jesus very much (*Matthew 26:6-13; Luke 7:36-50;*
John 12:1-11). She was lost in her sins but found forgiveness
in Jesus. She was poor in this world but gained a reward in
heaven. She was humbled in life but honored for her actions.

The Gospel of John says this woman was Mary the sister
of Martha and Lazarus (*John 11; 12:1-11*). It is also possibly
this woman was Mary Magdalene who became a follower of
Jesus (*Luke 8:1-3*) and was the first person to see the resurrected Jesus (*Matthew 28:1; Mark 16:1, 9; Luke 24:10; John 20:1,*
18). Was Mary Magdalene the sister of Martha and Lazarus?

Read *Psalm 42*, which encourages us to turn toward God
and seek his Word, presence and love.

DAY 37

While they were eating, Jesus took bread, gave thanks and broke it, and gave it to his disciples, saying, "Take it; this is my body."

Then he took the cup, gave thanks and offered it to them, and they all drank from it. "This is my blood of the covenant, which is poured out for many," he said to them. "I tell you the truth, I will not drink again of the fruit of the vine until that day when I drink it anew in the kingdom of God."

When they had sung a hymn, they went out to the Mount of Olives.

Mark 14:22-26

Jesus shares his last meal with his followers, which is call the *Passover* or *Seder Meal* (*Exodus 12:1-30*). It is a meal to remember how God delivered the Jewish people from slavery to freedom. It is a meal of joyful celebration and reverent reflection. It is an offering of thanksgiving to the God of goodness and grace. It is a sign of divine hospitality, friendship and blessing.

In church we call this meal by many names: The Last Supper; The Lord's Supper; Eucharist (thanksgiving); Mass (to send); Communion (fellowship); Covenant Meal; Sacrament (sacred mystery); Ordinance (duty); and Breaking Bread. It is a time of sharing in the grace and goodness of God and of affirming our faith in Jesus. We remember what God has done; we remember what he is doing; and we remember what God promised to do.

Read *Psalm 43*, which is similar to the preceding, which asks God for light and truth.

DAY 38

They went to a place called Gethsemane, and Jesus said to his disciples, "Sit here while I pray." He took Peter, James and John along with him, and he began to be deeply distressed and troubled. "My soul is overwhelmed with sorrow to the point of death," he said to them. "Stay here and keep watch."

Going a little farther, he fell to the ground and prayed that if possible the hour might pass from him. "Abba, Father," he said, "everything is possible for you. Take this cup from me. Yet not what I will, but what you will."

Mark 14:32-36

Jesus humbled himself to the will of God and to the death before him. Jesus knew his death would bring life to all creation. It was not easy; nor was it quick. Jesus was betrayed by one of his followers (*Mark 14:43*); arrested by the Jewish leaders (*Mark 14:46-47*); taken to the Sanhedrin (*Mark 14:53*); condemned to death and beaten (*Mark 14:64-65*); handed over to the Roman governor (*Mark 15:1*); tried by Pilate (*Matthew 27:11-14*); sent to Herod for review (*Luke 23:6-12*); declared innocent by Pilate (*John 18:38*); switched for Barabbas (*Matthew 27:15-23*); beaten by the Roman soldiers (*John 19:1-3*); mocked as the king of the Jews (*John 19:4-15*); presented to be crucified (*Luke 23:24-25*); mocked again (*Matthew 27:27-31*); and led to Golgatha, which is also called Calvary (*Mark 15:20*).

Read *Psalm 44*, which is a prayer for the followers of Jesus facing persecution and hardship.

DAY 39

It was the third hour when they crucified him. The written notice of the charge against him read: THE KING OF THE JEWS. They crucified two robbers with him, one on his right and one on his left. Those who passed by hurled insults at him, shaking their heads and saying, "So! You who are going to destroy the temple and build it in three days, come down from the cross and save yourself!"
Mark 15:25-30

The Stations of the Cross

First Station:
Jesus is Condemned to Death
(Mark 14:61-64)

Second Station:
Jesus Carries his Cross
(John 19:14-17)

Third Station:
Jesus Falls the First Time
(John 15:18-20)

Fourth Station:
Jesus Meets his Afflicted Mother
(no reference; see *John 19:25-27*)

Fifth Station:
Simon of Cyrene Helps Jesus to Carry his Cross
(Mark 15:20-22)

Sixth Station:
Veronica Wipes the Face of Jesus
(no reference; see *Matthew 25:37-40*)

Seventh Station:
Jesus Falls the Second Time
(no reference; see *Isaiah 53:4-6*)

Eighth Station:
>Jesus Meets the Women of Jerusalem
>*(Luke 23:27-28)*

Ninth Station:
>Jesus Falls a Third Time
>(no reference; see *Psalms 118:25-28)*

Tenth Station:
>Jesus Is Stripped of his Clothes
>*(Matthew 27:34-35)*

Eleventh Station:
>Jesus Is Nailed to the Cross
>*(Luke 23:33-34; John 19:18)*

Twelfth Station:
>Jesus Dies on the Cross
>*(Luke 23:44-46; John 19:30b)*

Thirteenth Station:
>The Body of Jesus Is Taken Down From the Cross
>*(John 19:33-34, 38a)*

Fourteenth Station:
>Jesus Is Laid in the Tomb
>*(Matthew 27:59-60)*

Read *Psalm 45*, which tells about the coming Jesus into the world with truth, grace, power and love.

PSALM 46

God is our refuge and strength,
an ever-present help in trouble.
Therefore we will not fear, though the earth give way
and the mountains fall into the heart of the sea,
though its waters roar and foam
and the mountains quake with their surging.
There is a river whose streams
make glad the city of God, the holy place where
the Most High dwells.
God is within her, she will not fall;
God will help her at break of day.
Nations are in uproar, kingdoms fall;
he lifts his voice, the earth melts.
The LORD Almighty is with us;
the God of Jacob is our fortress.

Come and see what the LORD has done,
the desolations he has brought on the earth.
He makes wars cease to the ends of the earth.
He breaks the bow and shatters the spear;
he burns the shields with fire.
He says, "Be still, and know that I am God;
I will be exalted among the nations,
I will be exalted in the earth."
The LORD Almighty is with us;
the God of Jacob is our fortress.

DAY 40

So Joseph bought some linen cloth, took down the body,
wrapped it in the linen, and placed it in a tomb cut out of rock.
Then he rolled a stone against the entrance of the tomb. Mary
Magdalene and Mary the mother of Jesus saw where he was laid.
   Mark 15:46-47

Jesus died upon the cross and was buried. His cross connected God to humanity by the great exchange of grace for our sin. Jesus became human and died so that humans could become like God and live. His cross connected heaven to earth. The kingdom of God now was in the hearts of those who had faith. This gives the world hope. His cross connected death to resurrection and brought redemption to suffering. This was an act of love. The grave could not hold him, and death could not keep him. His cross, his death, his resurrection changed everything.

And Can It Be?

> And can it be that I should gain
> An interest in the Savior's blood?
> Died He for me, who caused His pain —
> For me, who Him to death pursued?
> Amazing love! How can it be,
> That Thou, my God, shouldst die for me?
> Amazing love! How can it be,
> That Thou, my God, shouldst die for me?
>
>   Charles Wesley,
>   Traditional

Read *Psalm 47*, which declares the resurrection of Jesus and the victory of the followers of God.

DAY 41

"Don't be alarmed," he said. "You are looking for Jesus the Nazarene, who was crucified. He has risen! He is not here. See the place where they laid him. But go, tell his disciples and Peter, 'he is going ahead of you into Galilee. There you will see him, just as he told you.' Trembling and bewildered, the women went out and fled from the tomb. They said nothing to anyone, because they were afraid.
Mark 16:6-8

Resurrection Appearances

1. Appeared to Mary Magdalene — *John 20:14-16; Mark 16:9-11*
2. Appeared to other women — *Matthew 28:8-10*
3. Appeared to Peter — *Luke 24:34; 1 Corinthians 15:5*
4. Appeared to the Emmaus disciples — *Luke 24:13-31; Mark 16:12,13*
5. Appeared to the 10 — *Luke 24:36; John 20:19*
6. Appeared to the 11 — *John 20:26; 1 Corinthians 15:5; Mark 16:14*
7. Appeared to the seven — *John 21:1-14*
8. Appeared on the Galilee mountain — *Matthew 28:16-17; Mark 16:15-18*
9. Appeared to the 500 — *1 Corinthians 15:6*
10. Appeared to James — *1 Corinthians 15:7*
11. Appeared at the Ascension — *Luke 24:44-53; Mark 16:19; Acts 1:6-11*
12. Appeared to Stephen — *Acts 7:56*
13. Appeared to Paul — *1 Corinthians 15:8*

Read *Psalm 48*, which is a prayer of thanksgiving, praise and worship. It tells the Word of God will last forever.

DAY 42

After the Lord Jesus had spoken to them, he was taken up into heaven and he sat at the right hand of God. Then the disciples went out and preached everywhere, and the Lord worked with them and confirmed his word by the signs that accompanied it.
Mark 16:19-20

The Great Miracle of the Resurrection — *1 Corinthians 15:5-58*
1. The Resurrection is the centerpiece of the Gospel — *vv. 1-6*
2. The Resurrection is the beginning of the end — *vv. 12-28*
3. The Resurrection is the hope we have in this world — *vv. 29-34*
4. The Resurrection is the recreation of humanity — *vv. 35-44*
5. The Resurrection is the Christlikeness we bear — *vv. 45-49*
6. The Resurrection is the way we enter the next world — *v. 50*
7. The Resurrection is the great mystery — *v. 51*
8. The Resurrection is the second coming — *vv. 52-53*
9. The Resurrection is the victory over death — *vv. 54-57*
10. The Resurrection is the reason we stand firm — *v. 58*

Read *Psalm 49*, which warns the world not to trust in money or power but to seek the redeeming love of God.

Psalm 50

The Mighty One, God, the LORD,
speaks and summons the earth
from the rising of the sun to where it sets.
 From Zion, perfect in beauty, God shines forth.
 Our God comes and will not be silent;
a fire devours before him,
and around him a tempest rages.
 He summons the heavens above,
and the earth, that he may judge his people:
 "Gather to me this consecrated people,
who made a covenant with me by sacrifice."
 And the heavens proclaim his righteousness,
for he is a God of justice.
 "Listen, my people, and I will speak;
I will testify against you, Israel: I am God, your God.
 I bring no charges against you
concerning your sacrifices or concerning
your burnt offerings, which are ever before me.
I have no need of a bull from your stall or
of goats from your pens, for every animal of the
forest is mine, and the cattle on a thousand hills.
 I know every bird in the mountains,
and the insects in the fields are mine.
 If I were hungry I would not tell you,
for the world is mine, and all that is in it.
 Do I eat the flesh of bulls
or drink the blood of goats?
 "Sacrifice thank offerings to God,
fulfill your vows to the Most High,
and call on me in the day of trouble;
 I will deliver you, and you will honor me."
But to the wicked person, God says:
 "What right have you to recite my laws

or take my covenant on your lips?
    You hate my instruction
and cast my words behind you.
    When you see a thief, you join with him;
you throw in your lot with adulterers.
    You use your mouth for evil and harness
your tongue to deceit.
    You sit and testify against your brother
and slander your own mother's son.
    When you did these things and I kept silent,
you thought I was exactly like you.
    But I now arraign you
and set my accusations before you.
    "Consider this, you who forget God,
or I will tear you to pieces, with
no one to rescue you:
    Those who sacrifice thank offerings honor me,
and to the blameless I will show my salvation."

Chronological Tables of Rulers During New Testament Times

Roman Emperors

27 B.C.–A.D. 14	Augustus
A.D. 14-37	Tiberius
A.D. 37-41	Caligula
A.D. 41-54	Claudius
A.D. 54-68	Nero
A.D. 68-69	Galba; Otho; Vitellius
A.D. 69-79	Vespasian
A.D. 79-81	Titus
A.D. 81-96	Domitian

Herodian Rulers

37-4 B.C.	Herod the Great, king of the Jews
4 B.C.–A.D. 6	Archelaus, ethnarch of Judea
4 B.C.–A.D. 39	Herod Antipas, Tetrarch of Galilee and Perea
4 B.C.–A.D. 34	Herod Agrippa I, from 37 to 44 king over the former tetrarchy of Philip, and from 41 to 44 over Judea, Galilee and Perea
A.D. 37–44	Herod Agrippa II, king over the former tetrarchy of Philip and Lysanias, and from 56 (or 61) over parts of Galilee and Perea

Procurators of Judea after the Reign of Archelaus to the Reign of Herod Agrippa I

A.D. 6-8	Coponius
A.D. 9-12	M. Ambivius
A.D. 12-15	Annius Rufus
A.D. 15-26	Valerius Gratus
A.D. 26-36	Pontius Pilate
A.D. 37	Marullus
A.D. 37-41	Herennius Capito

Procurators of Palestine from the
Reign of Herod Agrippa I to the Jewish Revolt

A.D. 44-about 46	Cuspius Fadus
A.D. about 46-48	Tiberius Alexander
A.D. 48-52	Ventidius Cumanus
A.D. 52-60	M. Antonius Felix
A.D. 60-62	Porcius Festus
A.D. 62-64	Clodius Albinus
A.D. 64-66	Gessius Florus

New Testament Affirmations of Faith

First Things — *1 Corinthians 15:3-5*

For what I received I passed on to you as of first impor-
tance: that Christ died for our sins according to the Scriptures,
that he was buried, that he was raised on the third day accord-
ing to the Scriptures, and that he appeared to Cephas, and
then to the Twelve.

Conviction — *Romans 10:8-13*

But what does it say? "The word is near you; it is in your
mouth and in your heart," that is, the message concerning
faith that we proclaim: If you declare with your mouth, "Jesus
is Lord," and believe in your heart that God raised him from
the dead, you will be saved. For it is with your heart that you
believe and are justified, and it is with your mouth that you
profess your faith and are saved. As Scripture says, "Anyone
who believes in him will never be put to shame." For there is
no difference between Jew and Gentile — the same Lord is
Lord of all and richly blesses all who call on him, for, "Every-
one who calls on the name of the Lord will be saved."

Humility — *Philippians 2:5-11*

In your relationships with one another, have the same mindset as Christ Jesus:

Who, being in very nature God,
did not consider equality with
God something to be used to his own advantage;
rather, he made himself nothing
by taking the very nature of a servant,
being made in human likeness.

And being found in appearance as a man,
he humbled himself
by becoming obedient to death —
even death on a cross!

Therefore God exalted him
to the highest place
and gave him the name that is
above every name, that at
the name of Jesus every knee should bow,
in heaven and on earth and under the earth,
and every tongue confess that Jesus Christ is Lord,
to the glory of God the Father.

Godliness — *1 Timothy 3:16*

Beyond all question, the mystery from which true godli-
ness springs is great:
He appeared in the flesh,
was vindicated by the Spirit,
was seen by angels,
was preached among the nations,
was believed on in the world,
was taken up in glory.

Faithfulness — *2 Timothy 2:11-13*

Here is a trustworthy saying:
If we died with him,
we will also live with him;
if we endure,
we will also reign with him.
If we disown him,
he will also disown us;
if we are faithless,
he remains faithful,
for he cannot disown himself.

Resurrection — *Ephesians 5:8-14*

For you were once darkness, but now you are light in the Lord. Live as children of light (for the fruit of the light consists in all goodness, righteousness and truth) and find out what pleases the Lord. Have nothing to do with the fruitless deeds of darkness, but rather expose them. It is shameful even to mention what the disobedient do in secret. But everything exposed by the light becomes visible — and everything that is illuminated becomes a light. This is why it is said:

> *"Wake up, sleeper,*
> *rise from the dead,*
> *and Christ will shine on you."*

Glory — *Romans 11:33-36*

Oh, the depth of the riches of the
wisdom and knowledge of God!
How unsearchable his judgments,
and his paths beyond tracing out!
"Who has known the mind of the Lord?
Or who has been his counselor?"
"Who has ever given to God,
that God should repay them?"
For from him and through him
and for him are all things.
To him be the glory forever! Amen.

The Apostles' Creed

I believe in God the Father Almighty,
Maker of heaven and earth;
And in Jesus Christ His only Son our Lord;
Who was conceived by the Holy Spirit,
Born of the Virgin Mary, suffered under Pontius Pilate,
Was crucified, dead, and buried; He descended into Hades;
The third day He rose again from the dead;
He ascended into heaven and sitteth on the
right hand of God, the Father Almighty;
From thence He shall come to judge the quick and the dead.
I believe in the Holy Spirit,
the holy catholic* church,
The communion of saints,
the forgiveness of sins,
The resurrection of the body,
and the life everlasting. Amen.

*"catholic" refers to universal church

The Nicene Creed

We believe in one God, the Father, the Almighty, maker of heaven and earth, of all that is seen and unseen.

We believe in one Lord, Jesus Christ, the only Son of God, eternally begotten of the Father, God from God, Light from Light, true God from true God, begotten, not made, one in Being with the Father. Through him all things were made. For us men and for our salvation he came down from heaven: by the power of the Holy Spirit he was born of the Virgin Mary, and became man.

For our sake he was crucified under Pontius Pilate, he suffered, died, and was buried. On the third day he rose again in fulfillment of the Scriptures; he ascended into heaven and is seated at the right hand of the Father. He will come again in glory to judge the living and the dead, and his kingdom will have no end.

We believe in the Holy Spirit, the Lord, the giver of life, who proceeds from the Father and the Son. With the Father and the Son he is worshiped and glorified. He has spoken through the Prophets. We believe in one holy catholic* and apostolic Church. We acknowledge one baptism for the forgiveness of sins. We look for the resurrection of the dead and the life of the world to come. Amen.

*"catholic" refers to universal church

BIO

The Reverend Dr. Jeffrey P. Johnson is the superintendent of Mid-America Conference of the Free Methodist Church. He has served the Lord for 22 years as a pastor and missionary. As executive director for Men's Ministries International, he travels around the world teaching on evangelism and discipleship. He serves Global China Ministries, World Methodist Council Executive Committee, Wesley Commission, FMC-USA Board of Administration and Greenville College. His wife, Dr. Yasmin Johnson, is a professor of nursing at Oklahoma Baptist University, and they have two children, Ian Wesley and Isabella Anna Pauline.

Jeff has traveled throughout Asia and also lived in China for three years. He conducts Schools of Discipleship for churches interested in making disciples and promoting community renewal. He has ministered in more than 70 countries and oversees works in Guatemala and the Middle East.

Jeff earned a B.A. in history and an M.A. in education from Oral Roberts University and a doctorate in spiritual formation from George Fox Evangelical Seminary. He is an oblate in the Order of St. Benedict connected to St. Gregory's Abbey and University in Shawnee, Oklahoma.

Erin Smith is the administrator to the Mid-America Conference and the Midwest City Free Methodist Church. She is also the worship leader for the church. She is the conference secretary of the Mid-America Conference. Erin earned a Bachelor of Musical Arts from Oklahoma Baptist University. Her husband, the Reverend Jeremy Smith (Free Methodist elder), is a hospice chaplain, and they have two children, Caleb and Jacob.

CPSIA information can be obtained at www.ICGtesting.com
Printed in the USA
LVOW07s1338230215

427980LV00005B/7/P